Lisa Mäntler

Marca Mode v Adidas AG

Lisa Mäntler

Marca Mode v Adidas AG

ECJ Case C-425/98 – Confusion

ScienciaScripts

Imprint

Cover image: www.ingimage.com

This book is a translation from the original published under ISBN 978-3-639-48703-9.

Publisher:
Sciencia Scripts
is a trademark of
Dodo Books Indian Ocean Ltd. and OmniScriptum S.R.L publishing group

120 High Road, East Finchley, London, N2 9ED, United Kingdom
Str. Armeneasca 28/1, office 1, Chisinau MD-2012, Republic of Moldova, Europe
Managing Directors: Ieva Konstantinova, Victoria Ursu
info@omniscriptum.com

Printed at: see last page
ISBN: 978-620-9-69200-0

Table of Contents

CHAPTER 1 4

CHAPTER 2 9

CHAPTER 3 17

CHAPTER 4 31

CHAPTER 5 40

CHAPTER 6 42

Bibliography 43

Introduction

The subject of this paper, which takes as its starting point the 'Marca Mode' case—a trade mark case from the year 2000—is the examination of certain issues arising from the adoption of the First Council Directive 89/104/EEC of 21 December 1988 to approximate the laws of the Member States relating to trade marks (OJ 1989, L 40/1)[1] ,[2]

The aim of the Directive was to harmonise trade mark protection within the European Union. The chosen form of the Directive, which granted Member States a not insignificant degree of discretion in its implementation, as well as problems that existed from the outset due to the use of different terms in the individual language versions, gave rise to a number of ambiguities which subsequently had to be clarified at European Union level through preliminary ruling proceedings.

The specific nature of trade mark protection and the differing interests that must be taken into account when deciding each individual case have resulted in a multitude of judgments in which individual terms of the Trade Mark Directive have been repeatedly redefined and clarified. It was not until 27 March 2013 that the European Commission presented a proposal for a recast of the Trade Mark Directive. It remains to be seen where these efforts will lead.

This paper is based on the handling of the issue since the year 2000 and an extract from the decisions of the ECJ. In particular, the paper examines the specific features of the protection of well-known trade marks, explaining the difference from the protection of non-well-known trade marks , and the development of the interpretation of 'Section 10(2) of the Austrian Trade Mark

[1] Hereinafter referred to as: 'Trademark Directive' or 'Directive'.
[2] Hereinafter: 2008/95/EC; new Trade Mark Directive.

Act'[3] ,[4] and 'Article 5(2) of the Trade Mark Directive'[5] .

In its opinion on the European Commission's proposal for a recast of the Trade Mark Directive, GRUR advocated harmonising the various language versions of the Directive in line with the English version, so that in future there would be no further divergent interpretations of the term 'likelihood of confusion' as set out in Article 5(1)(b) of the Directive. Furthermore, in addition to the mandatory wording of Article 5(2) of the Directive – concerning the protection of a well-known trade mark – GRUR also welcomes the alignment of this very paragraph of Article 5 with the ECJ's 2003 'Zino Davidoff' judgment[6] , which is also discussed in detail.[7]

---

[3] Hereinafter referred to as: "Trademarks Act".
[4] See point 2. e.
[5] See point 1. b.
[6] See point 4.
[7] *Kunz-Hallstein, Loschelder*, GRUR's opinion on the European Commission's proposal for a recast of the Trade Mark Directive, GRUR 2013, 800.

CHAPTER 1

The leading case: Marca Mode CV v Adidas AG (C-425/98) 'Confusion in trade mark law'

a. Facts of the case

The decision in question (C-425/98 – 'Marca Mode CV v Adidas AG – Likelihood of confusion in trade mark law') of the European Court of Justice (ECJ) from 2000 is based on the facts that the company 'Marca Mode CV'[8] , with its registered office in Amsterdam (Netherlands) had offered sportswear for sale at its Dutch branch featuring two or three parallel vertical stripes, and the companies 'Adidas AG'[9] , based in Herzogenaurach (Germany), and 'Adidas Benelux BV'[10] , based in Etten-Leur (Netherlands) sought to prohibit the sale of these garments on the grounds that, by featuring these two or three stripes on the garments, 'Marca Mode' was infringing their protected three-stripe figurative mark, which was registered with the Benelux Trademark Office and for which 'Adidas Benelux BV' held the exclusive licence in the Benelux countries.

Both the court of first instance, namely the President of the Rechtbank Breda, and the court of second instance in the Netherlands, namely the Gerechtshof's-Hertogenbosch, upheld 'Adidas's' claim for an injunction.

"Marca Mode" then lodged an appeal in cassation with the "Hoge Raad"[11] . In this appeal, the company emphasised that the Court of Appeal had misapplied the relevant provision of Article 13(A)(1)(b) of the 'Uniform Benelux Trademark Law'[12] , because the decision was based solely on the finding that there was a

---

[8] Hereinafter referred to as: "Marca Mode CV" = "Marca Mode".
[9] Hereinafter in this paper: "Adidas AG" and "Adidas Benelux BV" = "Adidas".
[10] Hereinafter in this paper: "Adidas AG" and "Adidas Benelux BV" = "Adidas".
[11] Supreme Court of the Netherlands.
[12] Hereinafter: "Benelux Trade Marks Act".

risk that the relevant public might mentally associate the disputed signs with the registered trade mark. Citing the ECJ judgment "Sabel"[13] from 1997, "Marca Mode" argued that the Court of Appeal should have based its decision, pursuant to Article 5(1)(b) of the Trade Mark Directive, on the finding that a likelihood of confusion actually existed and was not merely presumed.

The Hoge Raad, however, took the view that, having regard to the 'Sabel' judgment, the distinctive character inherent in the 'Adidas' trade mark or arising from its reputation rendered the finding of a likelihood of association unnecessary, and that the judgment of the court of second instance should therefore not be set aside.

Furthermore, the Hoge Raad held that this interpretation of Article 5(1)(b) in conjunction with Article 5(2) of the Trade Mark Directive was compatible with well-known trade marks, as the latter provision allows the legislative bodies of the individual EU Member States to grant protection to well-known trade marks against the use of similar signs even where the goods are entirely different, provided that there is no likelihood of confusion.

Given that the Hoge Raad evidently harboured doubts as to the correctness of its own interpretation of the 'Sabel' judgment, it stayed the proceedings and, pursuant to Article 267 TFEU (formerly Article 234 EC), referred the following question to the ECJ for a preliminary ruling. The purpose of this was to clarify how Article 5(1)(b) of the Trade Mark Directive should be interpreted, namely in particular whether the provision could be interpreted as mean , *'that in the event*

1. *where a trade mark possesses distinctive character either intrinsically or by virtue of acquired reputation, and*
2. *a third party, without the consent of the trade mark proprietor, uses a sign in the course of trade for goods or services identical or similar to those for which the trade mark is registered, which corresponds to the trade mark to such an extent that there is a possibility of an association being made,*

the trade mark proprietor may, by virtue of his exclusive right, prohibit that third party from using the sign if, given the distinctive character of the trade mark, it cannot be ruled out

[13] ECJ 11 November 1997, Case C-251/95 – Sabel v Puma = ECR 1997, I-6191.

that this mental association may lead to confusion?"[14]

b. Legal background

The specific issue to be assessed is Article 5 ('Rights arising from the trade mark') of[15] (1)

1 (b) and Article 5(2) of the Trade Mark Directive:

> *'(1) The registered trade mark confers an exclusive right on its proprietor. This right permits the proprietor to prohibit third parties from using the trade mark in the course of trade without his consent*
>
> *(a) -*
> *b) from using a sign in the course of trade without his consent, where, because of the identity or similarity of the sign with the trade mark and the identity or similarity of the goods or services covered by the trade mark and the sign, there is a likelihood of confusion on the part of the public, which includes the likelihood that the sign will be mentally associated with the trade mark;*
>
> *(2) Member States may also provide that the proprietor is entitled to prohibit third parties from using, in the course of trade and without his consent, a sign identical with or similar to the trade mark in relation to goods or services which are not similar to those for which the trade mark is registered, where that sign is well known in the Member State concerned and where such use takes unfair advantage of, or is detrimental to, the distinctive character or the reputation of the trade mark without due cause.*[16]

These provisions of the Trade Mark Directive were transposed by the legislative bodies of the

Netherlands as follows, through Article 13A(1)(b) and Article 13A(1)(c) of the Benelux

Trademark Act:

> *'Without prejudice to the application of the general law of tort, the trade mark proprietor may, by virtue of his exclusive right, oppose*
>
> *a) -*
> *b) any use in the course of trade of the trade mark or a sign similar thereto for goods other than those for which the trade mark is registered, or for similar goods, where there is a likelihood that the public will mentally associate the sign with the trade mark;*
> *c) any use in the course of trade, without due cause, of a trade mark known in the Benelux territory or of a sign similar thereto for goods which are not similar to*

---

[14] ECJ 22 June 2000, Case C-425/98, para. 18 – Marca Mode – ÖBl 2000, 282 = wbl 2000, 236.

[15] Austria transposed the aforementioned Article 5 of the Trade Mark Directive into national law in the course of the 1992 (BGBl 773/1992) and 1999 (BGBl I 111/1999) amendments to trade mark law, through Section 10(1)(2) and (2) of the 'Trade Mark Protection Act'.

[16] Directive 89/104/EEC; Trade Mark Directive.

those for which the trade mark is registered, where such use takes unfair advantage of, or is detrimental to, the distinctive character or the reputation of the trade mark."[17]

c. Legal consequence

The ECJ ultimately ruled that the interpretation of the 'Sabel' judgment set out in point 2.1 is not applicable to the present case of 'Marca Mode v Adidas' and therefore rejected the question referred by the Hoge Raad regarding the interpretation of Article 5(1)(b) of the Trade Mark Directive[18] . In order to prohibit a third party from using a sign similar to the protected sign, it is therefore not sufficient that there is a possibility of a mental association leading to confusion; rather, it must be proven that such a mental association actually exists, even if the protected trade mark, the 'Adidas' three-stripe figurative mark, possesses distinctive character either intrinsically or by virtue of acquired distinctiveness. If one interprets Article 5(1)(b) of the Directive, as cited in point 2.2, according to its wording, it follows that the phrase 'risk of association' is intended to further define the term 'risk of confusion' and that the two concepts cannot be considered alternatives. For the provision in Article 5(1)(b) of the Trade Mark Directive to fulfil its protective function, there must therefore always be positive evidence of a likelihood of confusion.[19]

However, the reputation of a trade mark is significant in that trade marks which, due to their reputation, possess a high degree of distinctiveness enjoy more comprehensive protection than trade marks with a lower degree of distinctiveness.[20] This follows from the case law of the ECJ in the 'Sabel' case, according to which the existence of a likelihood of confusion must be assessed comprehensively, taking into account all relevant circumstances of the

---

[17] By Protocol of 2 December 1992, which entered into force on 1 January 1996.
[18] Paragraph 2 of Article 5 of the Trade Mark Directive was rightly not examined by the ECJ, as the statements made by 'Adidas' regarding the interpretation of the scope of application of this paragraph were not included by the Hoge Raad in its request for a preliminary ruling to the Court of Justice and no corresponding request was formulated.
[19] ECJ 29 September 1998, Case C-39/97, para. 18 – Canon = ÖBl 1999, 105.
[20] ECJ 29 September 1998, Case C-39/97, para. 18 – Canon =ÖBl 1999, 105.

individual case.[21] The comprehensive assessment of the likelihood of confusion implies an interdependence between relevant factors, such as the degree of similarity between the signs and the degree of similarity between the goods designated by them, and the reputation of the allegedly infringed trade mark.[22] Accordingly, where there is a lesser degree of similarity between the goods but a high degree of similarity between the trade marks, a likelihood of confusion may be established provided that the earlier trade mark can demonstrate a high degree of recognition.[23] However, the mere recognition of a trade mark is not sufficient to presume the existence of a likelihood of confusion simply because there is a potential risk of an association in the strict sense.

---

[21] ECJ 11 November 1999, Case C-251/95, para. 22 – Sabel/Puma =ÖBI 1998, 106 =wbl 1998, 34.
[22] ECJ 29 September 1998, Case C-39/97, para. 17 – Canon =OBI 1999. 105.
[23] ECJ 22 June 2000, Case C-425/98, para. 40 – Marca Mode =ÖBI 2000, 282 =wbl 2000, 236 with reference to ECJ 29 September 1998, Case C-39/97, para. 19 – Canon =ÖBI 1999, 105.

CHAPTER 2

Legal Basis

a. The Trade Mark Directive

The Trade Mark Directive, which aimed to harmonise the trade mark laws of the Member States of the European Union and to reduce differences between individual national rights of protection, was based on the Community's competence to establish a single internal market, as enshrined in Article 114(1) TFEU (formerly Article 95 TEC). From a legal policy perspective, it was intended to further develop trade mark law and thereby reduce conflicts between nationally limited rights of protection.[24] It was not the aim of the Trade Mark Directive to completely harmonise the trade mark laws of the individual Member States. The focus was therefore solely on harmonising those legal provisions governing the proper functioning of the internal market, restrictions on the free movement of goods and services, and the distortion of competition within the Common Market. These included rules on the acquisition and maintenance of trade marks and the resulting legal consequences, namely the protection conferred by the trade mark. Important legal provisions not affected by the harmonisation were, on the one hand, the procedural provisions of trade mark law and, on the other hand, the protection of unregistered signs. All Member States were obliged to transpose the Directive into national law within a specified period.[25]

Legal disputes must therefore continue to be assessed exclusively in accordance with the individual legal provisions transposed into national law . Where provisions of trade mark law apply, care must be taken when

---

[24] *Meyer*, German and French trade mark law following the transposition of the First Trade Mark Directive (Directive 89/104/EEC), GRUR Int 1996, 593.
[25] *Grünzweig*, Austrian Trade Mark Law (6th ed. 2011) Introduction, para. 3.

interpreting them in a specific case to determine whether they are harmonised provisions under the Trade Mark Directive or independent national legal provisions.[26] As the Directive covers only parts of trade mark law, the procedural rules in the trade mark protection laws of the individual EU Member States in particular are still subject to very significant differences.

However, in the event of any doubts regarding interpretation in the harmonised area, national authorities are bound by the case law and legal opinions of the ECJ in accordance with the principle of interpretation in conformity with the directive.

Thus, the case law of the ECJ is not only of great significance for the interpretation of primary law. Within the framework of the preliminary ruling procedure, the Court also provides further clarification of provisions contained in directives. In doing so, it indirectly exerts a major influence on the application and interpretation of the individual national trademark laws.[27] Consequently, should a national court of last instance in a pending case encounter a question relevant to the decision, the answer to which requires the interpretation of, inter alia, a European directive, it must stay the proceedings in accordance with Article 267 TFEU and refer the question to the ECJ for a preliminary ruling. This obligation to refer ensures that national legal provisions are interpreted, as far as possible, in the light of the wording and purpose of the underlying directive, thereby ensuring a uniform interpretation of Community law.

---

[26] *Grünzweig*, Austrian Trade Mark Law (6th ed. 2011) Introduction, para. 4; *Fercher* in Wiebe (eds.), Competition and Intellectual Property Law (2010) 78 et seq.; ECJ *Jacobs* 27 January 2000, Case C-425/98, para. 3 – Marca Mode [ECR 2000 I-4864].

[27] *Grünzweig*, Austrian Trade Mark Law (6th ed. 2011) Introduction para. 3, *Fercher* in Wiebe (ed.), Competition and Intellectual Property Law (2010) 79.

b. Issues relating to the background of European law / The history of the Directive

Although the national trade mark laws of the EU Member States and the 'Austrian Trade Mark Act' are based on the Trade Mark Directive, the enactment and, in some cases, even the literal transposition of the Directive by the respective national legislatures does not guarantee that all future legal issues will be assessed and interpreted uniformly across the individual Member States; certain legal provisions and concepts have evolved historically in the individual countries and have been interpreted and independently developed by national courts over many years. Even if supposedly traditional legal provisions remain part of national laws following the transposition of the Directive, the fact that these provisions now have a European legal background means that they must no longer be interpreted purely at the national level, as before, but against the backdrop of Community law. To complicate matters further, as already mentioned, not all provisions of national trade mark laws are covered by harmonisation. This leads to frequent ambiguities or conflicting viewpoints regarding the interpretation of European legal concepts when deciding legal issues. However, these must be interpreted uniformly across the EU and thus also when applying the individual national trade mark laws.[28] In order to achieve the objective of resolving existing doubts in a legally binding manner, national courts refer matters to the ECJ under the preliminary ruling procedure. The ECJ acts as a body for further training and clarification regarding the interpretation of European legal concepts in accordance with the directives.

The case of 'Marca Mode v Adidas', which forms the starting point for this paper and has already been described in detail in section 1, is an example of how conflicting concepts in individual Member States can lead to differences of

[28] *Engin-Deniz,* MSchG^2 (2010) § 10 131.

interpretation and resulting legal disputes. The ECJ's clarification and further development of the concepts of 'likelihood of confusion', 'degree of recognition' and 'distinctiveness' of a trade mark are also central to the present case. All these terms are used in Article 5(1)(b) and (2) of the Trade Mark Directive (provisions on trade mark rights).Which criteria are necessary to determine the 'likelihood of confusion' or the 'distinctiveness' of a trade mark, and whether these are present in a specific case, is therefore a matter for national case law or, ultimately, the case law of the ECJ.[29] The content of these legal concepts cannot always be clearly deduced from the abstract wording of the Directive alone.

c. The problem of differing wording in the various language versions of the Trade Mark Directive

Although the tenth recital of the preamble to the Trade Mark Directive uses the term 'risk of confusion' in several places, the word 'risk' has not been used in all language versions of the Directive. The English version, for example, speaks of 'likelihood', which translates as 'probability', whereas the Dutch version refers to the 'possibility' of confusion and mental association. All other versions (including the German version) use either the term 'Gefahr' or 'Risiko'.[30]

Consequently, the chosen term was also incorporated into the respective national trademark laws. These differing formulations and the varying degrees of emphasis placed upon them provide a further explanation for why, despite the harmonisation of trademark laws, differing legal views were able to develop and crystallise in the individual EU countries. In my view, the concept of the 'possibility' of confusion is the one that can be interpreted most broadly and

---

[29] *Guggenbichler* in Kucsko (ed.), marken.schutz (2006) 291.
[30] ECJ *Jacobs* 27 January 2000 Case C-425/98, para. 8 – Marca Mode = ECR 2000 I-4864.

therefore offers the greatest possible scope of protection. This is followed by the term 'probability' as used in the English version, then the concept of 'danger' and finally that of 'risk'. These divergences have also contributed to the ECJ acquiring far-reaching significance within the framework of trade mark law.

d. The problem of differing interpretations of the scope of trade mark protection in the EU Member States and the impact on Article 5(1)(b)

The wording of Article 5(1)(b) of the Trade Mark Directive,

> ***"where there is a likelihood of confusion, which includes the likelihood that the sign will be mentally associated with the trade mark"***[31]

states that the 'likelihood of confusion' also encompasses 'association in the mind'. This wording represents a compromise between the differing interpretations of national trademark concepts that came to light during the drafting of the Trademark Directive. Following lengthy negotiations in Brussels between the representatives of the Benelux countries and those of the other Member States, the aforementioned Article 5 was agreed. Whilst the negotiating partners from the Benelux countries, following the model of the Uniform Benelux Trademark Act, wished to maintain very extensive trademark protection by insisting on the formulation of 'risk of mental association' even in the absence of a 'risk of confusion' instead of the term 'risk of confusion', the other delegations called for adherence to the concept of 'likelihood of confusion in the traditional sense', namely as a mere risk of association, in order to preserve the brand's function of indicating origin.[32] *Verkade* described the

---

[31] Directive 89/104/EEC; Trade Mark Directive.
[32] *Fezer,* First principles of the ECJ on the likelihood of confusion under trade mark law – or: 'How far does the big cat leap?', NJW 1998, 713 ff.

phrase "likelihood of confusion including mental association" as "linguistic nonsense"[33] , whilst the Federal Court of Justice (BGH) expressed itself somewhat more cautiously, referring to "ambiguous wording"[34] . Even when interpreted in the narrowest possible sense, the expression "mental association" always encompasses far more than the "likelihood of confusion". For the former term undoubtedly also encompasses cases of reputation exploitation, reputation impairment and dilution, in which no deception as to origin is required. This inherently contradictory legal wording cannot be resolved even by a very broad interpretation of the "likelihood of confusion".[35]

Due to the issues outlined above, serious interpretation problems for the future were already predicted before the deadline for transposing the Directive had expired. Particularly in cross-border cases, where differing interpretations of the term 'likelihood of confusion' can be decisive for the use and scope of protection of even well-known trade marks, far-reaching problems arose soon after the transposition of the Directive into national trade mark laws. In particular, the case of the global corporation ' ' ('Adidas'), which forms the basis of this paper, has shown that the purpose of the Directive, namely the harmonisation of trade mark law within the internal market, is reaching its limits due to the divergent wording of national laws. The conflict, which was already inevitable, concerning the traditionally established 'Adidas' trademark in the neighbouring Benelux countries has clearly demonstrated the need for a uniform understanding of the concept of a trademark and the scope of its protection.

---

[33] *Verkade,* Harmonisation of national trade mark law in the EEC: Benelux States, GRUR Int 1992, 96, concurring with *Sack,* Special protection for well-known trade marks, GRUR 1995, 89.

[34] Federal Court of Justice (BGH) GRUR 1996, 198 ff., 200 (3.) – Leaping big cat.

[35] *Sack*, Special protection for well-known trade marks, GRUR 1995, 89, *Sack*, 'Double identity' and 'mental association' in the new German and European trade mark law, GRUR 1996, 667.

d. Transposition of the Directive into Austrian law

e.

As already explained above under point 1. b., the necessary amendments to the Austrian Trade Mark Protection Act were made in the course of the 1992 (BGBl 1992/773) and 1999 (BGBl 1999/111) amendments to trade mark law in order to comply with the obligation to harmonise the Member States' legislation on trade marks. Article 5 of the Trade Mark Directive, on which this paper is based, was transposed into Section 10 of the Trade Mark Act as follows:

> *'(1) Subject to the preservation of prior rights, the registered trade mark confers on its proprietor the exclusive right to prevent third parties from using, in the course of trade,*
>
> 1 ...
> 2 *to use, in the course of trade, a sign identical with or similar to the trade mark in relation to goods or services identical with or similar to those covered by the trade mark (Section 10a), where there is a likelihood of confusion on the part of the public, which includes the likelihood that the sign will be mentally associated with the trade mark.*
>
> 3 *2) The proprietor of a registered trade mark is also entitled to prohibit third parties from using, in the course of trade and without his consent, a sign identical or similar to the trade mark for goods or services (Section 10a) which are not similar to those for which the trade mark is registered, if the trade mark is well known in Germany and the use of the sign takes unfair advantage of, or is detrimental to, the distinctive character or the reputation of the trade mark without due cause. The earlier trade mark must have been well known by the date of application for the later trade mark at the latest, or, where applicable, by the date of priority or the date on which seniority is based, or at the time the later other right to a sign arose."*[36]

This shows that the Austrian legislature has largely adhered to the wording of the Directive. Key terms of the Trade Mark Directive have been incorporated verbatim into the national provisions. The legislative bodies of the Federal Republic of Germany have also, in transposing the aforementioned Article into Section 14 of the German 'Trade Mark Act'[37] , used terms that largely correspond to those of the Directive.

The reason for this was, on the one hand, to avoid the risk of the Trademark

[36] Federal Law Gazette 260/1970 as amended by Federal Law Gazette I 111/1999.
[37] Hereinafter referred to as "MarkenG".

Directive being implemented incorrectly and, on the other hand, to ensure that the Austrian provisions corresponded as closely as possible in substance to the fundamental European principles laid down by the Directive. It should be emphasised at this stage that, in its wording of Section 10(2) of the Austrian Trade Marks Act (MSchG), the Austrian legislature made use of the option provided by the Directive to grant extended protection to well-known trade marks under specific circumstances (see Section 10(2) MSchG).[38] Article 5(1)(b) and (2) of the Trade Mark Directive and its interpretation and application by national and European case law will be the focus of the remainder of this paper. In doing so, I rely primarily on Austrian literature, commentaries, textbooks and journals.

---

[38] Ninth recital of the Trade Mark Directive.

CHAPTER 3

Issues at the level of European law / the interpretation of the Directive by the ECJ

In order to address in greater detail the problems arising from the different linguistic formulations of the Directive, the key terms of the Directive in their various versions will be examined in more detail below.

a. Definitions of terms using the Austrian Trade Mark Act as an example, taking into account differing interpretations in other Member States

aa. The concept and function of the trade mark

A 'registered trade mark' is a trade mark within the meaning of the Trade Marks Act. The current wording of Section 1 of the Trade Marks Act, which defines the concept of a trade mark, was amended to bring it into line with the Trade Mark Directive as part of the 1999 amendment to trade mark law. The legislator does not define the term 'sign' in detail, but merely illustrates types of signs that may be entered in the register of signs. These include, amongst others, the classic cases such as words, including personal names, images and letters. The Trade Mark Directive is based on a very broad concept of a trade mark. The scope of 'signs' eligible for protection can therefore be extended to all types, provided that they can be represented graphically and the 'sign' is capable of distinguishing goods and services of different manufacturers from one another, i.e. possesses distinctive character.[39] When assessing whether a trade mark is eligible for protection, the focus is solely on the theoretical possibility of distinction, i.e. on an abstract capacity to distinguish, .[40] The

[39] *Fercher* in Wiebe (ed.), Competition and Intellectual Property Law (2010) 79 ff.
[40] *Hauer* in Kucsko (ed.), marken.schutz (2006) 4.

actual eligibility for protection is only assessed when examining the conditions for registration.[41] In addition to the aforementioned distinguishing function of a trade mark, its origin function is now, according to the established case law of the Supreme Court, its primary function.[42] This can also be inferred from Recital 10 of the preamble to the Trade Mark Directive.[43] In this context, the trade mark is intended to guarantee to the consumer or end user the identity of origin of the goods or services designated by it, by enabling them to distinguish those goods or services from goods or services of other origins without any likelihood of confusion.[44] The trade mark thus identifies a company's goods or services. By virtue of this identifying function, the trade mark serves to distinguish a company's goods or services from those of other companies.[45] Furthermore, the trade mark fulfils a function of trust, quality and guarantee, which can be derived from its function of indicating origin. This is intended to enable the consumer to rely on the quality expectations already associated with a trade mark and to ensure certain standards. Finally, the advertising function of a trade mark must be mentioned, as it often conveys an advertising message to the consumer. Since some Member States grant 'well-known trade marks' an extended scope of protection and the case law of the ECJ also grants 'well-known trade marks' extended protection under specific circumstances, this function must also be recognised and taken into account by the Trade Marks Act.[46]

bb. Selected relative grounds for refusal

Before a trade mark application can be filed, it must be checked whether there

[41] See point 3. a. bb.
[42] *Grünzweig*, Austrian Trade Mark Law (4th ed. 2008) § 1 margin note 21.
[43] Recital 10 states: 'The purpose of the protection afforded by the registered trade mark is, in particular, to ensure the trade mark's function as an indicator of origin (...)'.
[44] ECJ 29 September 1998, Case C-39/97, para. 15 – Canon = ÖBl 1999. 105. *Schumacher* in Kucsko (ed.), marken.schutz (2006) 212.
[45] *Fezer*, MarkenR^4(2009) § 3 para. 11.
[46] *Grünzweig*, Austrian Trade Mark Law (4th ed. 2008), § 1, para. 30 et seq.

are any absolute or relative grounds for refusal pursuant to Section 4 of the Trade Marks Act. Whilst the existence of an absolute ground for refusal completely precludes the registration of a trade mark, a relative ground for refusal may be overcome by obtaining and — [41] See point 3. a. bb.
evidence of established reputation, and the 'sign' may ultimately be registered after all. Section 4(1)(3), (4) and (5) of the MSchG lists the relative grounds for refusal. Paragraph (3) generally stipulates that non-distinctive 'signs' are excluded from registration. Paragraphs 4 and 5, on the other hand, regulate specific cases of lack of distinctiveness, namely, on the one hand, in paragraph 4, purely descriptive signs and indications, and, on the other hand, in paragraph 5, generic terms.

bba. Distinctiveness and the need to keep terms free

The standard of assessment used to determine whether a sign possesses distinctive character has been significantly relaxed since the 1999 amendment to the Trade Marks Act. Distinctiveness therefore means that the trade mark is capable of identifying the goods (services) for which registration is sought as originating from a particular undertaking and thus of distinguishing those goods (services) from those of other undertakings.[47] As already mentioned above, a sign that lacks distinctiveness is excluded from entry in the trade mark register. This is stipulated in Section 4(3) of the Trade Marks Act (MSchG), which, in contrast to the other two relative grounds for refusal (Sections 4(4) and 4(5)), also functions as a catch-all provision .[48] However, even a low degree of distinctiveness is sufficient to permit the registration of a sign.[49]

The purpose of the relative ground for refusal under Section 4(3) of the MSchG

---

[47] ECJ 18 June 2002, Case C-299/99, para. 26 – Philips Shaver = ÖBl 2003/15 with further references.
[48] *Grünzweig*, Austrian Trade Mark Law (4th ed. 2008) § 4 para. 8b.
[49] *Grünzweig*, Austrian Trademark Law (7th ed. 2012) § 4 para. 8d.

is to ensure a certain need for availability in the public interest, i.e. to guarantee the free availability of signs.[50] It should be noted that the concept of the need to keep signs available does not constitute a ground for refusal listed in the Trade Marks Act, but the provisions of subparagraphs 3, 4 and 5 are based on a need to keep the signs listed therein available in the public interest. This is intended to prevent individual terms used by the general public from being monopolised by a

trademark owner.[51]

Whether a trade mark possesses distinctive character is determined on the basis of a prognosis. In doing so, it must be examined whether the 'relevant public' can distinguish the goods or services of the trade mark in question from those of competitors when selecting a product. The 'relevant public' comprises not only those persons who are prepared to purchase the goods for which the sign under examination is claimed, but also traders and competitors.[52] In the case of everyday consumer goods, this assessment of registrability is based on the perception of an average consumer who is reasonably well-informed, observant and circumspect, characterised by a good level of education and a high degree of perceptiveness.[53]

bbb. Purely descriptive signs

A descriptive sign within the meaning of Section 4(1)(4) of the Trade Marks Act (MSchG) is defined as a sign which uses indications that, in the understanding of the 'relevant public', may designate goods and services in common

---

[50] *Fercher* in Wiebe (ed.), Competition and Intellectual Property Law (2010) 91.
[51] *Grünzweig,* Austrian Trade Mark Law (3rd ed. 2007) § 4 margin note 25.
[52] *Asperger* in Kucsko (ed.), marken.schutz (2006) 107 ff., *Mutz* in Kucsko (ed.), marken.schutz (2006) 177.
[53] *Asperger* in Kucsko (ed.), marken.schutz (2006) 108.

parlance. In short, it is a sign that provides a 'statement of quality'.[54] A sign is not to be classified as a descriptive sign if it merely contains indications of a certain quality, without, however, specifically describing the goods or services designated by it.[55]

An example of a purely descriptive sign is, for instance, 'car care' in relation to car care[56] [57] , whereas 'Top-Cat' for cat litter is not descriptive.[57]

bc. Recognition in trade

The term 'recognition in trade' refers to the situation where a significant proportion of the relevant domestic public (e.g. consumers, traders, competitors) recognises a sign as a clear indication of a specific undertaking. When determining whether a sign has acquired a reputation, a distinction is made between the concepts of the degree of recognition, the degree of distinctiveness and the degree of association. Whilst the mere recognition of a sign does not in itself indicate that it has acquired a reputation, as no connection has yet been established with specific goods or services, the degree of distinctiveness is decisive. It is precisely this that indicates whether a sign is recognised within the 'relevant public' as an indication of a specific undertaking, or of a specific product or service. The degree of association, on the other hand, indicates the extent to which the undertaking with which the sign is associated is known by name.[58]

If a sign cannot, a priori, be admitted for registration due to an inherent lack of distinctiveness pursuant to Section 4(1)(3), due to its exclusively descriptive character pursuant to Section 4(1)(4), or because it gives the impression of

---

[54] *Grünzweig*, Austrian Trade Mark Law (4th ed. 2008) § 4 margin note 8.
[55] OPM 28 September 2005, Om 8/05 – Fabric Conditioner – PBI 2006, 65 with further references, *Fercher* in Wiebe (ed.), Competition and Intellectual Property Law (2010) 93 ff.
[56] *Grünzweig*, Austrian Trade Mark Law (4th ed. 2008) § 4 margin note 67d.
[57] *Engin-Deniz*, MSchG[2] (2010) § 4 99.
[58] *Fercher* in Wiebe (ed.), Competition and Intellectual Property Law (2010) 95 ff.

being a generic term pursuant to Section 4(1)(5) of the Trade Marks Act (MSchG), Section 4(2) of the Trade Marks Act still offers the applicant the possibility of obtaining registration of the desired sign by providing evidence. This evidence refers to the fact that, through use no later than the filing date or priority date, the sign has acquired the missing distinctive character (= established reputation) within the 'relevant public' in Austria. In other words, this means that a sign may still be registered despite the existence of a relative ground for refusal, provided that the applicant for the desired trade mark provides positive evidence of established reputation during the registration proceedings.[59] In order for the competent authority to confirm the reputation of a sign, the applicant must submit impeccable documentation that records the genuine perception of the 'relevant public'. Such documentation must in any case include advertising materials, customer testimonials, opinion polls, chamber of commerce reports, sales figures, balance sheets and sales contracts.[60] The required degree of recognition in the relevant public depends on how little distinctive character a sign possesses. It is all the higher the less distinctive character there is and the greater the need to keep the sign free for use. Case law rejects fixed percentages that dictate whether recognition in the relevant public has been proven. Where the degree of recognition exceeds 50% within the 'relevant public', there is generally considered to be a high degree of recognition.[61]

For example, in a ruling, the Federal Court of Justice (BGH) required that the combination of the colours grey and magenta, which by its very nature does not serve to indicate commercial origin, must demonstrate a level of recognition exceeding the 50% threshold. The Higher Regional Court of Hamburg followed the BGH's view and deemed the 47% level of recognition for the colour

---

[59] *Mutz* in Kucsko (ed.), marken.schutz (2006) 177.
[60] *Mutz* in Kucsko (ed.), marken.schutz (2006) 179 ff.
[61] *Grünzweig*, Austrian Trade Mark Law (7th ed. 2012) § 4 margin note 146 et seq.

combination orange and black to be insufficient.[62]

b. Right of exclusion pursuant to Section 10 of the Trade Marks Act

Section 10 of the Trade Marks Act (MSchG) can be described as the central provision of the Act. This provision defines the scope of protection afforded to a trade mark and grants the trade mark proprietor an absolute right of exclusion.[63] The trade mark proprietor is thus able, under certain conditions, to prohibit a third party from 'using'[64] his trade mark in the course of trade without his consent.

bb. Protection against confusion of the trade mark (Section 10(1)(2) MSchG)

The use of a sign identical to the trade mark for the same goods or services ('double identity') in the course of trade without the consent of the trade mark proprietor infringes his rights pursuant to Section 10(1)(1) of the Trade Marks Act. Whether there is a likelihood of confusion is not to be taken into account in this context. However, the situation is different where both the conflicting signs and the goods or services in question are not identical but merely similar. In this case, trade mark protection applies only if there is a likelihood of confusion, which includes the risk that the sign will be mentally associated with the trade mark.[65] However, it is sufficient that the use of the disputed sign by third parties could lead to confusion with the protected trade mark, rather than

---

62 *Fezer*, MarkenR^4 (2009) § 4 para. 123.
63 *Grünzweig*, Austrian Trade Mark Law (7th ed. 2012) § 10 margin note 1.
64 The term 'use' is defined in Section 10a of the Trade Marks Act.
65 *Schumacher* in Kucsko (ed.), marken.schutz (2006) 200.

that confusion has actually occurred in a specific case.[66] As already indicated in the explanation of the facts under point 1 and further under points 2. c and d, it is often not easy to determine whether there is a likelihood of confusion within the meaning of Section 10(1)(2) of the Trade Marks Act.

Whether there is a likelihood of confusion is a legal question which the court or the judge must decide comprehensively, taking into account all the circumstances of the individual case.[67,68] . In exceptional cases, should the judge's general life experience prove insufficient, findings of fact may be relied upon.[69] The concept of likelihood of confusion is a concept under European law, which the ECJ has further clarified in various judgments, thereby establishing a number of principles.[70] It therefore exists where the public might believe that the goods or services in question originate from the same undertaking (likelihood of confusion in the narrow sense) or , at most, from undertakings economically linked to one another (likelihood of confusion in the broader sense). The likelihood of confusion in the narrow sense can be further subdivided and is deemed to exist where, on the one hand, the public confuses the signs themselves (direct likelihood of confusion) and, on the other hand, where the relevant public does not directly confuse the signs but mistakenly attributes them to the same undertaking (indirect likelihood of confusion). The existence of a likelihood of confusion therefore always entails an impairment of the trademark's function of indicating origin.[71] It should be noted that, for a likelihood of confusion to exist, an indirect likelihood of confusion is sufficient.[72]

The comprehensive assessment referred to above means that, when

---

[66] *Grünzweig*, Austrian Trade Mark Law (5th ed. 2010) § 10 para. 6.

[67] ECJ 11 November 1999, Case C-251/95. Para. 22 – Sabel v Puma = ÖBl 1998. 106 = wbl 1998. 34.

[68] See point 1. c.

[69] *Schumacher* in Kucsko (ed.), Marken.Schutz (2006) 201.

[70] See point 1. c.

[71] *Schumacher* in Kucsko (ed.), marken.schutz (2006) 208 ff, *Fercher* in Wiebe (ed.), Wettbewerbsund Immaterialgüterrecht (2010) 98.

[72] *Engin-Deniz*, MSchG^2 (2010) § 10 132.

assessing the likelihood of confusion, the interplay between the relevant factors must be taken into account.[73] In particular, the degree of recognition of the trade mark on the market and the degree of similarity between the two signs and between the goods or services they designate must be assessed.[74] Accordingly, a lower degree of similarity between the goods may be offset by a higher degree of similarity between the signs and the degree of recognition of the earlier trade mark, and may lead to a likelihood of confusion.[75]

For a comprehensive assessment of the likelihood of confusion, it is particularly important to consider the effect the signs have on the 'relevant public'[76] for this type of goods.[77] In this context, the level of attention paid by the individual members of the relevant public may vary. This depends on the specific situation and will, for example, be comparatively low when purchasing everyday consumer goods. Consequently, the likelihood of confusion is greater due to the lower level of attention than, for example, when purchasing a car, where the purchaser is generally more attentive and better informed.[78]

bc. Protection of a well-known trade mark (Section 10(2) MSchG)

Section 10(2) of the Trade Marks Act (MSchG) provides for the extended protection of a well-known trade mark, which goes further than that regulated in Section 10(1) of the MSchG, as it is also applicable outside the scope of similar goods and services. This protection extending beyond the scope of similarity is necessary because well-known trade marks also have an impact

[73] *Grünzweig*, Austrian Trade Mark Law (5th ed. 2010) § 10 para. 13.
[74] ECJ 11 November 1999, Case C-251/95, para. 22 – Sabel v Puma = ÖBl 1998, 106 = wbl 1998, 34.
[75] ECJ 29 September 1998, Case C-39/97, para. 18 – Canon =ÖBl 1999, 105.
[76] In the case of low-value everyday consumer goods, the average consumer must be taken into account.
[77] *Schumacher* in Kucsko (ed.), marken.schutz (2006) 214 ff.
[78] *Fercher* in Wiebe (ed.), Competition and Intellectual Property Law (2010) 100.

across sectoral boundaries and today possess significant economic value.[79] Pursuant to Article 5(2) of the Trade Mark Directive, the provision of Section 10(2) of the Trade Marks Act was incorporated into the Trade Marks Act as part of the 1999 trade mark law amendment. Granting special protection to well-known trade marks is not mandatory within the limits provided for in the Directive, but optional. It is left to the Member States themselves to decide whether to incorporate this provision into their respective national trade mark laws or not to make use of it.[80]

The legal concept of '[81] ' of a well-known trade mark is not defined in detail in the statutory provisions. The interpretation of this term, or the establishment of criteria for its determination, is therefore a matter for the courts.[82] Whether a trade mark is to be classified as well-known must be assessed taking into account both qualitative and quantitative criteria. The quantitative criterion is met as soon as the trade mark is known to a significant section of the 'public'[83] affected by the goods or services covered by the trade mark. When assessing the reputation of a trade mark, the specific circumstances of the individual case must always be taken into account; no fixed percentages have been established. From a qualitative perspective, it must be considered whether the trade mark has a 'reputation' that could be exploited or impaired. It is not entirely clear whether reputation always presupposes qualitative aspects, such as a 'good reputation'.[84] The reputation of the earlier trade mark must exist by the date of filing of the later trade mark at the latest and, except in the case of a trade mark that is well known, must always be proven by the party claiming

---

[79] *Guggenbichler* in Kucsko (ed.), marken.schutz (2006) 283 ff.
[80] It should be noted that most EU Member States have made use of this option.
[81] *Fezer*, MarkenR^4 (2009) § 14 para. 756.
[82] *Guggenbichler* in Kucsko (ed.), marken.schutz (2006) 291.
[83] Public = for everyday consumer goods, the brand must be well-known among the general public; for more exclusive goods, however, it must be well-known among the group that has an interest in these products.
[84] *Guggenbichler* in Kucsko (ed.), marken.schutz (2006) 295 with reference to *Fezer*, MarkenR^4 (2009) § 14 para. 767, *Ingerl/Rohnke*, MarkenG^3 (2010) § 14 para. 1338.

such reputation.[85]

In contrast to Section 10(1)(2) of the Trade Marks Act (MSchG), Section 10(2) provides protection even in the absence of a likelihood of confusion. However, the degree of similarity between the well-known trade mark and the sign must be such that the relevant public mentally associates the sign with the trade mark.[86]

A further prerequisite for the protection of the well-known trade mark is that one of the four grounds for infringement is satisfied. These acts of infringement include the unfair exploitation of reputation (= exploitation of reputation), the unfair impairment of reputation (= damage to reputation), the exploitation of distinctiveness (= exploitation of attention) and the e impairment of distinctiveness (= dilution). In addition to the criteria of the brand's reputation and the similarity of the signs, an element of unfairness must therefore also be present for the protective function of Section 10(2) of the Trade Marks Act to apply. The offence therefore extends into the realm of unfair competition.[87]

1 .) Exploitation of reputation: Here, the good reputation or positive image of a trademark is exploited in an unfair manner and commercially exploited for the benefit of the infringer. In this case, there is exploitation of reputation.[88]

2 .) Impairment of reputation: The offence of damage to reputation aims to ward off negative influences on a positive brand image and the diminishment of the appeal of a well-known brand. The aim here is to protect the positive image of a brand from another trademark owner using a similar or identical sign for goods of inferior quality.[89]

3 .) Exploitation of distinctiveness: This involves infringements of a trade

[85] *Fercher* in Wiebe (ed.), Competition and Intellectual Property Law (2010) 101 ff.
[86] *Grünzweig*, Austrian Trade Mark Law (7th ed. 2012) § 10, margin note 117 et seq.
[87] *Grünzweig*, Austrian Trade Mark Law (7th ed. 2012) § 10 margin note 118.
[88] *Guggenbichler* in Kucsko (ed.), marken.schutz (2006) 301.
[89] *Fercher* in Wiebe (ed.), Competition and Intellectual Property Law (2010) 102.

mark's distinctive character and promotional power. By using the well-known trade mark, the infringer draws the public's attention to themselves and their product; their aim is not to 'free-ride' on the trade mark's reputation, but to use it to gain a communicative advantage (= eye-catching). Unlike in the two scenarios mentioned above, the well-known trademark does not need to have a good reputation in this context. Exploitation of attention thus provides a catch-all provision for all those cases in which the exploitation of reputation cannot be clearly established.[90]

4 .) Impairment of distinctive character: Dilution is understood as the reduction of the distinctive character and thus also of the advertising function of a well-known trademark through the use of an identical or similar sign by a third party. Given that the public often only subconsciously recalls the well-known trade mark, it is possible that they are persuaded to make a purchase solely through the mental association with the infringing sign. This can result in the distinctive character of a registered trade mark being diminished to such an extent that an exclusive, immediate mental association with the undertaking for which the trade mark was originally registered is no longer possible. The extent of protection against dilution depends on the degree of recognition of the trade mark and the degree of sectoral distance. The greater the sectoral distance between the products, the more the degree of recognition of the trade mark determines the level of protection. Particularly well-known trade marks also enjoy protection against dilution in respect of virtually all goods and services.[91]

c. The issue of Article 5(2) of the Trade Mark Directive

As has already been mentioned and explained in detail several times in the course of this paper, the interpretation of the Trade Mark Directive is ultimately the responsibility of the ECJ. It therefore also indirectly determines the

[90] *Grünzweig*, Austrian Trade Mark Law (7th ed. 2012) § 10 margin note 122.
[91] *Grünzweig*, Austrian Trade Mark Law (7th ed. 2012) § 10 margin note 122a.

interpretation of the respective national legal provisions in accordance with the Directive. The transposition of Article 5(2) of the Directive into national trade mark law is not mandatory, but optional. The Member States of the EU are therefore granted a degree of discretion in the transposition process, which does not entail any binding requirements for national trade mark law. Consequently, an interpretation of national law in conformity with the Directive is also ruled out in this area.[92]

In my view, it was inevitable that granting such leeway would rather quickly lead to ambiguities or differing conclusions regarding the assessment of the scope of protection of a well-known trade mark. One of the main objectives, namely the harmonisation of trade mark rights for registered trade marks across all EU Member States, was thus clearly missed. This scenario had already become apparent, amongst other things, in the 'Marca Mode' case[93] discussed above and remains a point of debate to this day.

In that very judgment from 2000, the Court of Justice of the European Union did not include the scope of application of Article 5(2) of the Trade Mark Directive in its review and therefore did not interpret it in detail. This was because the Hoge Raad of the Netherlands had ruled out its applicability in this case due to the lack of a difference in goods and had not taken it into account when formulating the question referred to the ECJ. Due to the limited scope of the question referred, the facts had to be subsumed under Article 5(1)(b) of the Directive and a decision had to be made on the basis of that provision as to whether protection should be granted to the 'Adidas mark'. The ECJ ultimately ruled against this, as even in the case of well-known trade marks, a likelihood of confusion must actually exist in order for the necessary elements of Article 5(1)(b) of the Trade Mark Directive to be fulfilled and for the provision to be applicable. All of this is subject to the condition that there is any similarity

---

92 *Sack,* Special Protection for Well-Known Trade Marks, GRUR 1995, 81.
93 See point 1. c.

between the goods at all. In other words, this means that the existence of a likelihood of an association (unlike in Article 5(2), where this is sufficient) is not enough to grant protection under Article 5(1)(b) of the Trade Mark Directive, and this is the case even if the trade mark possesses distinctive character.

In fact, the entire issue should properly have been subsumed under Article 5(2) from the outset in order to be able to discuss and cover the subject of the necessary mental association and the scope of protection for well-known trade marks . Due to the limited scope of the question referred, this was not possible in the 'Marca Mode' case. Nevertheless, there was no doubt that this question must be interpreted within the framework of paragraph 2, which expressly refers to the reputation of a trade mark. A literal interpretation of Article 5(2) of the Directive therefore leads to a different scope of protection for well-known trade marks.[94] Understandably, this type of interpretation soon met with criticism. Particularly where goods are similar, a well-known trade mark must be afforded protection against any exploitation or impairment not simultaneously associated with a likelihood of confusion.[95] In my view, this is justified, among other things, because the devaluation of a well-known trade mark in the area of similarity occurs more rapidly through the unauthorised use of a similar sign by a third party than would be the case in the absence of similarity of goods.[96] However, taking into account the wording of Article 5(2) of the Trade Mark Directive, this problem can only be resolved by analogy.[97,98]

---

[94] *Engin-Deniz*, MSchG[2] (2010) Section 10 161 et seq.
[95] *Guggenbichler* in Kucsko (ed.), marken.schutz (2006) 298.
[96] See point 4.
[97] *Koppensteiner*, Protection of well-known trade marks only in the absence of similarity of goods? =ecolex 2007, 696.
[98] *Ingerl/Rohnke*, MarkenG[3] (2010) § 14 para. 1282.

CHAPTER 4

The evolution of case law regarding Article 5(2) of the Trade Mark Directive and Section 10(2) of the Trade Marks Act over the years since the 'Marca Mode v Adidas' case

Since the landmark case, 'Marca Mode CV v Adidas AG – Confusion in trade mark law', the principles applicable at the time have evolved, and the individual terms of Article 5 of the Trade Mark Directive and Section 10 of the Trade Marks Act have been given a new meaning. The fact that Adidas's action for an injunction was dismissed in 2000 did not mean that the underlying issue had been definitively resolved. On the contrary, it became the subject of legal dispute once again in several subsequent legal proceedings and led to ever-changing approaches to interpreting the provisions on the protection of well-known trade marks.

In the years that followed, numerous requests for preliminary rulings were referred to the ECJ, through which Article 5(2) was defined in greater detail and the special protection afforded to well-known trade marks took on a clearer shape. This was precisely the case in the 'Zino Davidoff' judgment[99] of 9 January 2003. In response to the referral from the Federal Court of Justice (BGH), the scope of protection under Article 5(2) of the Trade Mark Directive was clarified, and it was held that, contrary to the wording of the provision, this should not be restricted to cases of dissimilarity of goods in order to do justice to the general scheme and the objective of the legislation. The ECJ thus clarified that, contrary to the wording of the Directive, protection must be granted to a well-known trade mark not only in cases of dissimilar goods, but also in cases of similar goods. By analogy, the provision has now been extended to cover cases where a sign identical or similar to a well-known trade mark ( ) is used by a third party for identical or similar goods and services,

[99] ECJ 09.01.2003, Case C-292/00 – Zino Davidoff =ÖBl 2003/55.

thereby unfairly prejudicing the reputation or distinctive character of the well-known trade mark.[100] The justification for the Court of Justice of the European Union ([101]) adopting a broader interpretation lies in the fact that the protection of a well-known trade mark is even more necessary in the case of the use of a sign for similar goods than in the case of its use for goods that are different.[102] In the 'Zino Davidoff' judgment, the ECJ further held that the provision of Article 5(2) of the Trade Mark Directive grants the individual Member States which have made use of the option to grant extended protection to well-known trade marks the power to extend the special protection of the well-known trade mark to the area of similarity of goods and services. However, it initially remained unclear whether this granting of protection was at the discretion of the respective Member State or whether it was mandatory.[103] Shortly afterwards, this very question was addressed in the 'Adidas Stripes II' decision[104] and ultimately answered by the ECJ. It emerged from this judgment that, provided Article 5(2) of the Directive had been transposed into national law, identical and similar goods or services must be afforded a scope of protection at least as broad as that afforded to dissimilar goods. It is therefore solely for the individual Member States to decide whether to grant extended protection to well-known trade marks at all, but not which circumstances are covered by this protection if they make use of the option granted.[105] Furthermore, this conclusion is supported by the fact that, in the 'Marca Mode' case discussed above, the ECJ held that the conditions of Article 5(1)(b) of the Directive are fulfilled, even in the case of well-known trade marks, only if there is positive evidence of a likelihood of confusion.[106]

---

[100] *Grünzweig,* Austrian Trade Mark Law (7th ed. 2012) § 10 para. 117b.
[101] See point 3. c.
[102] ECJ 9 January 2003, Case C-292/00, para. 12 – Zino Davidoff = ÖBl 2003/55.
[103] ECJ 23 October 2003, Case C-408/01 – Adidas Stripes II = ecolex 2004/175 = ÖBl-LS 2004/43 = wbl 2004/2.
[104] ECJ 23 October 2003, Case C-408/01 – Adidas Stripes II =ecolex 2004/175 =ÖBl-LS 2004/43 =wbl 2004/2.
[105] ECJ 23 October 2003, Case C-408/01, para. 20 – Adidas Stripes II =wbl 2004/2.
[106] *Grünzweig,* Austrian Trade Mark Law (7th ed. 2012) § 10 para. 117b.

The Supreme Court reached a similar conclusion in the 'Red Dragon' case, concurring with the European Court of Justice's view regarding the scope of protection of a well-known trade mark. It, too, extended the scope of protection to goods belonging to the same or identical categories. In its headnote, the Supreme Court even went so far as to state that, when a sign similar to a well-known sign is used for an identical product, it is reasonable to suspect unfair motives, as the possibility of reputation exploitation is obvious.[107] This therefore actually makes it easier for the proprietor of a well-known trade mark to enforce their rights.[108] This allows the conclusion that the exploitation of reputation, damage to reputation and dilution of well-known trade marks generally indicate illegality, and that this only ceases to apply if the competitor using the similar sign can invoke special circumstances justifying their conduct.[109]

In addition to the question of the similarity of the goods or services, an important decision was also made in the 'Adidas Stripes II' case regarding the necessary degree of similarity between the well-known trade mark and the sign. It should be noted here that, for the protection afforded by Article 5(2) of the Trade Mark Directive, it is sufficient that the degree of similarity between the well-known trade mark and the sign gives rise to a mental association between the two within the relevant public. Article 5(2) of the Directive therefore also applies even where there are circumstances that rule out any likelihood of confusion.[110]

A further question referred for a preliminary ruling in the 'Adidas Stripes II' case concerned the significance of the positioning of the 'Adidas stripes'. The fact that the relevant public perceives this stripe sign as a decoration does not preclude the protection of well-known trade marks granted by Article 5(2) of the

[107] Supreme Court 29 November 2005, 4 Ob 122/05b - Red Dragon =ecolex 2006/291.
[108] Supreme Court 29 November 2005, 4 Ob 122/05b, Commentary - Red Dragon =ecolex 2006/291.
[109] Supreme Court 29 November 2005, 4 Ob 122/05b – Red Dragon =ecolex 2006/291.
[110] ECJ 23 October 2003, Case C-408/01, para. 31 – Adidas Stripes II =wbl 2004/2, *Engin-Deniz*, MSchG[2] (2010) § 10 160.

Trade Mark Directive, provided that the degree of similarity between the trade mark and the sign is so pronounced that a mental association arises. When considering the two-stripe sign on the garments of the competing undertaking, a mental association within the meaning of the ECJ must be affirmed if, upon seeing these goods, the customer thinks of the Adidas company but realises that the product cannot be from Adidas.[111] A mental association is generally ruled out if, following an assessment of the facts by a national court, it is established that the relevant public perceives the conflicting sign merely as decoration (and therefore not as a trade mark).[112] In this regard, the national court must proceed on the basis of the overall impression that the conflicting sign creates on the average, reasonably well-informed, observant and circumspect member of the relevant public for the product group.[113]

Taking this into account, the Supreme Court ruled in the similar case of 'Puma Formstrip'[114] concerning the well-known sportswear brand Puma that the degree of similarity between the appliqués adorning the shoes and the registered trade mark was too remote to give rise to a mental association on the part of the relevant public and thus to exploitation of reputation, damage to reputation and/or dilution of the well-known trademark. The claimant should have provided evidence that the defendant, through the use of the disputed appliqué, exploited or damaged the reputation of its trademarks.[115] Decorations in the form of appliqués are not unusual on sports and leisure footwear and usually serve not only as an indication of a product's origin but also as a purely fashion-related attribute. However, the exclusive right of a trade mark proprietor is only infringed if the sign in question also serves as an indication

[111] *Winkhaus*, The Concept of Similarity of Signs in the Special Protection of Well-Known Trade Marks (PhD thesis, University of Tübingen 2009) 94.
[112] ECJ 23 October 2003, Case C-408/01, para. 38 et seq. – Adidas Stripes II =wbl 2004/2.
[113]Supreme Court 23 May 2006, 4 Ob 48/06x – Puma Formstrip =ÖBl 2008/15, *Engin-Deniz*, MSchG[2] (2010) § 30 316.
[114] Supreme Court 23 May 2006, 4 Ob 48/06x – Puma Formstrip =MR 2006, 270.
[115] Supreme Court 23 May 2006, 4 Ob 48/06x, para. 2 – Puma Formstrip =MR 2006, 270.

of origin and is not merely classified as a decoration.[116] Accordingly, protection of a trade mark under Article 5(2) of the Trade Mark Directive can only be refused if it is regarded as a mere ornament, because in that case it is naturally impossible to establish a mental connection with the registered trade mark.[117]

Both the Austrian Supreme Court in the 'Puma Formstrip' decision and the European Court of Justice in the 'Levi Strauss' decision, handed down shortly before[118], state that even in the case of well-known trade marks, a fair balance must be sought between the interests of the trade mark proprietor on the one hand and those of the public or other economic operators on the other.[119] The issue surrounding the scope of protection of trade marks which are merely descriptive or lack distinctiveness but were nevertheless registered because they have become established in the market, and their relationship to the need to keep certain terms free for general use, was once again the subject of discussion before the Hoge Raad of the Netherlands. On 21 February 2007, the Hoge Raad referred the matter to the ECJ for a final ruling, and the ECJ revisited the issues of the 'Adidas stripes', 'association in the mind of the consumer' and the 'likelihood of confusion' ( ) in its 'Adidas Stripes III' judgment[120].

This judgment sought to clarify whether the 'need to keep the mark free'[121] constitutes an assessment criterion capable of limiting the scope of protection of the absolute right of a trade mark proprietor. The provision ("limitation of the effect of the trade mark")[122] in Article 6(1)(b) of the Trade Mark Directive is an

[116] Supreme Court 23 May 2006, 4 Ob 48/06x, para. 2 – Puma Formstrip =MR 2006, 270, *Engin-Deniz*, MSchG² (2010) § 30 316.
[117] ECJ 23 October 2003, Case C-408/01 – Adidas Stripes II =ÖBl 2004/37 *(Kuchar)*.
[118] ECJ 27 April 2006, Case C-145/05 – Levi Strauss =ÖBl 2006/58 *(Gamerith)*.
[119] Supreme Court 23 May 2006, 4 Ob 48/06x, p. 83 – Puma Formstrip =ÖBl 2008/15.
[120] ECJ 10 April 2008, Case C-102/07 – Adidas Stripes III = 0Bl-LS 2008/155, = wbl 2008/151 = ecolex 2008/277 = ÖBl 2008/63.
[121] See point 3. a. bb. bba.
[122] Austria transposed the aforementioned Article 6(1)(b) of the Trade Mark Directive into domestic law through Section 10(3) of the 'Trade Mark Protection Act' as part of the 1992 (BGBl 773/1992) and 1999 (BGBl I 111/1999) amendments to trade mark law.

expression of the need to keep terms free and aims to ensure that the general public and all economic operators have the opportunity to use descriptive indications. However, as already mentioned above in point 3. a bb bba, the need to keep terms free does not constitute an independent limitation on the effect of the trade mark which is in addition to the limitations provided for in Article 6(1)(b) of the Trade Mark Directive. Consequently, a third party wishing to rely on the possible limitations on the effects of a trade mark listed in Article 6(1)(b) of the Trade Mark Directive, and subsequently on the need to keep the mark free for general use underlying that provision, must relate the indication used by them to a characteristic of the goods sold by the third party or the services provided by them.[123] In the present case, 'Adidas Stripes III', the defendants and the competitors of 'Adidas' considered themselves entitled to apply two parallel stripes to sports and leisure clothing without consent. They invoked the need to keep the public domain free. In their view, stripes and stripe motifs were merely signs which anyone should be free to use at any time.[124] In the present case, the ECJ found that the two-stripe motifs used by the defendant parties were purely decorative in nature and consequently did not indicate any characteristic of those goods. The fact that the disputed sign was to be classified merely as decoration was evident from the statements made by Adidas' competitors, which they themselves submitted to the Court.[125] Furthermore, the Court of Justice held in this judgment that the existence of a need to keep the field open does not constitute a criterion to be taken into account when assessing the likelihood of confusion, as the focus here must be on how the relevant public perceives the signs. Furthermore, with regard to the scope of protection of the well-known trade mark, the ECJ held that the need to keep the sign free is not a relevant criterion even when assessing whether

---

[123] ECJ 10 April 2008, Case C-102/07, para. 46 et seq. – Adidas Stripes III = ecolex 2008/277, = ÖBl 2008/63.
[124] http://www.kostenlose-urteile.de/EuGH_C-10207_EuGH-Die-drei-Adidas-Streifen-sind-vom-Markenrecht-geschuetzt.news5881.htm [20 September 2013].
[125] ECJ 10 April 2008, Case C-102/07, para. 48 et seq. - Adidas Stripes III = ÖBl 2008/63.

there is unfair impairment or exploitation of the reputation or distinctive character of a trade mark.[126]

The Austrian Supreme Court (OGH) also addressed the question of distinguishing between mere ornamentation and a protectable trade mark in a 2012 decision concerning 'Red Bull'. In its reasoning, it found that in the case in question, the blue/silver colour combination did not constitute a mere ornament but – precisely because of its renown – possessed an independently distinctive character. It follows that the use of even individual elements of this ornamentation can give rise to an association in the mind of the public. In its headnote, the Court even goes so far as to state that the assessment of public perception constitutes a question of law where everyday experience is sufficient for its evaluation.[127]

Taking into account the case law of the ECJ, can two-stripe motifs infringe the three-stripe motif of 'Adidas'?

The 'Adidas' case has clearly demonstrated that decisions in trade mark law are essentially case-by-case determinations. When assessing each set of facts, conflicting interests must be taken into account, including the protection of a trade mark, the free market economy, the need for competitors to have access to certain terms, and consumer associations. Even weak signs within the meaning of trade mark law can, by virtue of their renown, enjoy disproportionate protection. In individual cases, the protection afforded to a well-known trade mark is already so comprehensive that it becomes difficult to comprehend. As *Gamerith* aptly criticised in his commentary 'Adidasstreifen II' as early as 2003, the well-known 3-stripe sign of the company 'Adidas' in the original legal dispute consists, to a considerable extent, perhaps even predominantly, of a form that is dictated by the nature of the goods (sports and leisurewear) themselves or which confers significant value on the goods. In this

[126] ECJ 10 April 2008, Case C-102/07, pp. 308 et seq. – Adidas Stripes III = ÖBl 2008/63.
[127] Supreme Court 12 June 2012, 17 Ob 27/11m – Red Bull = ecolex 2012/412.

form, the trade mark is not only a distinguishing mark but also an important fashion attribute of the goods. The trade mark thus deprives competing companies and competitors of essential fashion design elements which are precisely typical of sports and leisure clothing. It is clear from the facts of the 'Adidas Stripes II' case that the company 'Adidas' not only claims these design elements for itself in a single version, but also asserts that the three-stripe motif must be protected in various sizes and colour combinations, provided that it always contrasts with the base colour of the garment. This almost all-encompassing protection was rightly criticised by *Gamerith*, who argued that the scope of protection of the three-stripe mark should be restricted in the event of a conflict, in the interests of balancing the competing interests.[128]

His concerns, raised as early as 2003, have since been confirmed by the ECJ in "Adidas Stripes III" to the effect that there are hardly any possibilities for competitors to use stripes – even if only as decoration – because the ECJ had firmly established that, despite its purely decorative nature, a sign bears such a similarity to a registered trade mark that the relevant public might believe the goods originate from the same undertaking or, where applicable, from economically linked undertakings.[129] Taken to the extreme, this would mean that parts of the sporting goods market could be permanently monopolised beyond the statutory terms of design protection. Unless the ECJ provides clarification to the contrary in the foreseeable future, 'variable figurative marks' would become permissible.[130]

In my view, this is correct, because not every combination of stripes evokes an association with the 'Adidas' trade mark in the mind of the average consumer. It is common practice in the market to design the seam of sports trousers in the

---

128 ECJ 23 October 2003, Case C-408/01, Commentary – Adidas Stripes II = ÖBl 2004/37 *(Gamerith)*.
129 ECJ 10 April 2008, Case C-102/07 – Adidas stripes III =ecolex 2008/277.
130 ECJ 10 April 2008, Case C-102/07, para. 311 – Adidas Stripes III = ÖBl 2008/63 *(Gamerith)*.

form of one or more stripes. In this context, it must suffice to protect only an exclusive three-stripe combination. The use of a two-stripe motif should therefore be permitted in the interests of undistorted competition within the Common Market, as envisaged by the Trade Mark Directive, and the associated balancing of interests of all parties involved (in particular trade mark proprietors, consumers and competitors).

CHAPTER 5

Relationship between trade mark law and the Unfair Competition Act (UWG) since the enactment of the Trade Marks Act (MSchG) in 1999

Until the introduction of Section 10 of the Trade Marks Act (MSchG), the scope of protection for well-known trade marks was governed by the Unfair Competition Act (UWG) and regulated within the scope of competition law.

Since then, due to the requirements of European law, the newly introduced Section 10 of the MSchG has provided the framework for issues relating to trade mark protection. Whether there remains scope for the application of competition law provisions on the protection of performance rights alongside the aforementioned provision is a matter of dispute.

Section 9 of the UWG continues to regulate the protection of business identifiers. This term is broader than the concept of a trade mark used in the MSchG and takes precedence over it, as it also encompasses, amongst other things, unregistered trade marks, names and company names as business identifiers within the meaning of the UWG.

Furthermore, the UWG does not require a competitive relationship to grant protection. However, actual use in the course of trade is also a prerequisite there. The provisions are also similar in that business identifiers, like trade marks, must possess distinctive character to fall within the scope of application. Within this framework, they are protected against the use of similar business identifiers by other undertakings if this gives rise to a likelihood of confusion.

It remains, however, a matter of dispute in what form the provisions coexist. The prevailing case law assumes that the Trade Marks Act provides an exhaustive regulation and grants protection under competition law only if such protection is denied under the Trade Marks Act.[131]

The Supreme Court, on the other hand, initially continued to grant protection under competition law alongside protection under trade mark law – still with reference to Article 5(2) of the Directive. It cannot be inferred from the admissibility of trade mark protection that the case law on the unconscionable exploitation of reputation is no longer applicable. In subsequent decisions, the Supreme Court left it undisputedly open as to whether, following the adaptation of the Trade Marks Act (MSchG) to the Trade Marks Directive, the legal protection of well-known trade marks is now to be assessed exclusively on the basis of the MSchG, or whether there remains scope for additional protection of such signs under competition law.[132]

---

[131] Federal Court of Justice 30 April 1998, I ZR 268/95 – Mac Dog = GRUR 1999, 161.
[132] *Guggenbichler* in Kucsko (ed.), marken.schutz (2006) 305, Supreme Court 9 March 1999, 4 Ob 35/99c – Boss Energy Drink 11 – ecolex 1999, 480 *(Schanda)*, Supreme Court 12 September 2001, 4 Ob 166/01t – Vogue – ÖBl 2003, 28.

CHAPTER 6

Summary

The aim of this paper was to demonstrate, using the 'Marca Mode' trademark case as a starting point, the difficulties that have arisen in the course of harmonising trademark protection in Europe. Even before the Trademark Directive was actually adopted, the background of European law and the history of its development gave rise to extensive discussions, which were based on differing understandings of terms and divergent interpretations of individual concepts across the Member States. Furthermore, the fact that a certain degree of discretion was granted in the implementation of the Directive, as well as the various language versions of the Directive, which contained differing terms, gave rise to a number of problems, some of which were discussed in greater detail. The focus of this work was on Article 5(1) and (2) of the Trade Mark Directive, in particular the terms 'likelihood of confusion' and 'likelihood of association' used therein, as well as the specific features of the protection afforded to well-known trade marks compared to non-well-known trade marks. In this context, the role of the ECJ was also highlighted, which, in the context of preliminary ruling proceedings, had to address and interpret numerous ambiguities at the level of European law. This remains the case today and leads to individual terms of the Trade Mark Directive being redefined time and again. To put an end to this seemingly endless process, the European Commission expressed its intention in 2013 to recast the Trade Mark Directive, incorporating the extensive case law of the ECJ.

Bibliography

Textbooks

WIEBE, Andreas (ed.): Competition and Intellectual Property Law (2010)

Commentaries

ENGIN-DENIZ, Egon: Trade Mark Protection Act and Other Provisions on Signs [2] (2010) 1323 pp

FEZER, Karl-Heinz: Trade Mark Law. Commentary on the Trade Marks Act, the Paris Convention and the Madrid Agreement. Documentation of national, European and international trade mark law [4] (2009) 2876 pp

GRÜNZWEIG, Clemens: Austrian, European and International Trade Mark Law. Practical Commentary on the Trade Mark Protection Act (2011), loose-leaf edition

INGERL, Reinhard/ ROHNKE, Christian: Trademark Act. Explanation of the Act on the Protection of Trademarks and Other Signs[3] . (2010)

KUCSKO, Guido (ed.): Trademark Protection. A Systematic Commentary on the Trademark Protection Act (2006) 1007 pp

Published dissertations

WINKHAUS, Amelie: The Concept of Similarity of Signs in the Special Protection of Well-Known Trade Marks (PhD thesis, University of Tübingen 2009) 193 pp

Articles in journals

FEZER, Professor Dr Karl-Heinz: Initial principles of the ECJ on the likelihood of confusion under trade mark law – or: 'How far does the big cat leap?', NJW 1998, 713

KOPPENSTEINER, Hans-Georg: Protection of well-known trade marks only in the absence of similarity of goods?, ecolex 2007, 696

KUNZ-HALLSTEIN, LOSCHELDER: GRUR's statement on the EU Commission for a recast of the Trade Mark Directive, GRUR 2013, 800

MEYER, Andreas: German and French trade mark law following the transposition of the First Trade Mark Directive (Directive 89/104/EEC), GRUR Int 1996, 592

SACK, Rolf: 'Double identity' and 'mental association' in the new German and European trade mark law, GRUR 1996, 663

SACK, Rolf: Special protection for well-known trade marks, GRUR 1995, 81

VERKADE, D.W. Feer: Harmonisation of national trade mark law in the EEC: Benelux countries, GRUR Int 1992, 92

Opinion

Opinion of Advocate General Jacobs of 27 January 2000, ECJ Case C-425/98 – Marca Mode

Websites used

http://www.kostenlose-urteile.de/EuGH_C-10207_EuGH-Die-drei-Adidas-Streifen-
are-protected-by-trademark-law.news5881.htm [accessed on 20 September

2013]

Case law index

1. ECJ

Name of the decision	Case number	Date	Reference	Mentioned on page...
Sabel v Puma	C-251/95	11 November 1997	ÖBl 1998, 106 =wbl 1998, 34	10, 13, 28, 29
Canon	C-39/97	29 September 1998	ÖBl 1999, 105	12, 13, 22, 29
Marca v Adidas	C-425/98	22 June 2000	ÖBl 2000, 282 =wbl 2000, 236	11, 13
Philips Electronics	C-299/99	18 June 2002	ÖBl 2003/15 et seq.	24
Zino Davidoff	C-292/00	09/01/2003	ÖBl 2003/55	35, 36
Adidas II	C-408/01	23 October 2003	ecolex 2004/175 =ÖBl-LS 2004/43 =wbl 2004/2 =ÖBl 2004/37	36, 37, 38, 39, 43
Levi Strauss	C-145/05	27 April 2006	ÖBl 2006/58	39
Adidas III	C-102/07	10 April 2008	ÖBl-LS 2008/155, =wbl 2008/151 =ccolex 2008/277 =ÖBl 2008/63	40, 41, 43

2nd Supreme Court – Decisions

Name of the decision	Case number	Date	Reference	Mentioned on page...
Boss Energy Drink II	4 Ob 35/99c	09/03/1999	ecolex 1999, 480	45
Vogue	4 Ob 166/011	12	ÖBl 2003, 28	45

		September 2001		
Red Dragon	4 Ob 122/05b	29 November 2005	ecolex 2006/291	37
Puma Formstrip	4 Ob 48/06x	23 May 2006	MR 2006, 270 = ÖBl 2008/15	38, 39
Red Bull	17 Ob 27/11m	12 June 2012	ecolex 2012/412	41

4. Federal Court of Justice – Decisions

Name of the decision		Date	Reference	Mentioned on page...
Leaping Big Cat		29 June 1995	GRUR 1996, 198	19
Mac Dog		30 April 1998	GRUR 1999, 161	44

3rd OPM – Decision

Name of the decision	Case number	Date	Reference	Mentioned on page...
Fabric Conditioner	Aug 2005	28 September 2005	PBl 2006, 65 mwN	25

Druck:
CPI Druckdienstleistungen GmbH
im Auftrag der
Kolibri 360 GmbH
Ferdinand-Jühlke-Str. 7
99095 Erfurt

Kolibri 360 GmbH
Ferdinand-Jühlke-Straße 7
99095 Erfurt, Deutschland
produktsicherheit@kolibri360.de